"ROSIE"
THE ROSE SPIDER

WRITTEN BY: TINA M. MACK

JUNE 14, 2004

WITH ILLUSTRATIONS BY:

TINA M. MACK

ILLUSTRATIONS INSPIRED BY:

MY GRANDSON, MASON.

BOOK DEDICATED TO:

MY SON, KYLE.

I LOVE YOU!

Copyright © 2004 Tina M. Mack

Rosie was a friendly spider who only wanted to be loved by someone. She searched high and she searched low, but all she could find were people who just didn't understand that spiders have feelings too. Everyone she came in contact with either ran away screaming or they tried to beat her with a broom or even worse; they would try to step on her with their shoes.

She knows that she is not the cuddliest creature and she may not fetch a ball when you throw it, but she's a great listener and she'd always be there for you when you need her. She'd also love you forever.

One fine morning she set out again looking for that perfect someone who she could play with and call friend. She didn't know it but this day was going to be her lucky day.

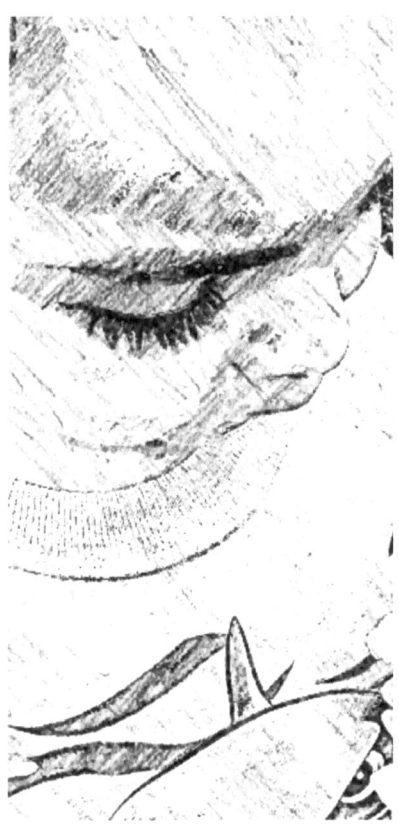

As Rosie shot out strands of web to swing from tree to tree singing and smiling like she always did when she was looking around, she saw the most unusual thing. She saw a young boy sitting in one of the trees, crying. She slowly walked under a leaf that was sitting right next to him. Being very careful not knowing what he'd do.

Rosie very softly asked; "Little boy, why are you crying"? The Little boy looked all around but didn't see anyone. He asked; "Who said that"? She soon replied, "I'm Rosie! I would come out, but you would only run away from me". The boy answered back; "Why would you say that"? Sounding very sad, Rosie replied; "I am a spider, a Rose spider". "Nobody ever seems to like me, because I look way too scary and I sort of freak them out". The little boy told her proudly; "I love spiders"! Rosie was so surprised that she almost fell out of the tree.

So, Rosie came out from under the leaf and for the first time, she felt proud to be a spider.

When the young boy saw her, he had a grin from ear to ear. Rosie looked up at him and she had the biggest grin, too. In fact, she almost started to cry. No one in her family would have ever guessed that she would ever find a human to be her friend.

The young boy politely introduced himself to Rosie. "Hello, my name is Kyle. It's a pleasure to meet you"! As Rosie added to that; "The pleasure is all mine".

Rosie asked; "Kyle, why were you crying"? Kyle replied; "I lost my best friend, Beacon. He was an old dog. I've known him my whole life. I am really going to miss him". Rosie warmly said; "I am very sorry for your loss, Kyle! I wish there was a way that I can make you feel better"! Then Rosie walked up Kyle's arm and up to his face and wiped his tears away.

Kyle looked at Rosie and said; "I know of some places that would make both of us feel better". So, Rosie sat on his shoulder as he climbed down from the tree. She could tell Kyle was a wonderful person and that they were going to have the best time.

And she was right...

Rosie never felt so alive before. She's actually playing with a boy who likes her for who she really is. It's like a fairy tale. As they're skipping along the sidewalk, they see the neighborhood park. Kyle asked; "Rosie, do you want to play on the playground with me"? She immediately replied; "Yeah, yeah, yeah"! Kyle took her on the slide, the monkey bars, and the swings. They swung so high that they were laughing so hard their cheeks started to hurt and their sides ached.

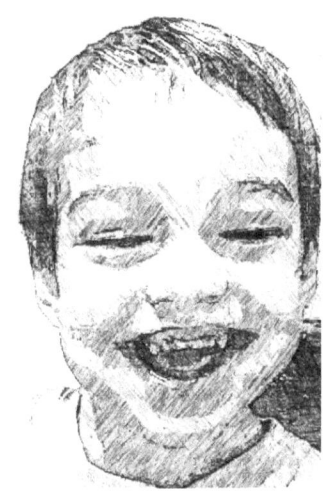

They made it just in time for the town's parade. This is Rosie's first parade. Well, actually being able to see the parade.

Rosie sat on Kyle's head so she could watch the parade with her new best friend. They waved to their favorite characters in the parade as they shared some cotton candy with each other.

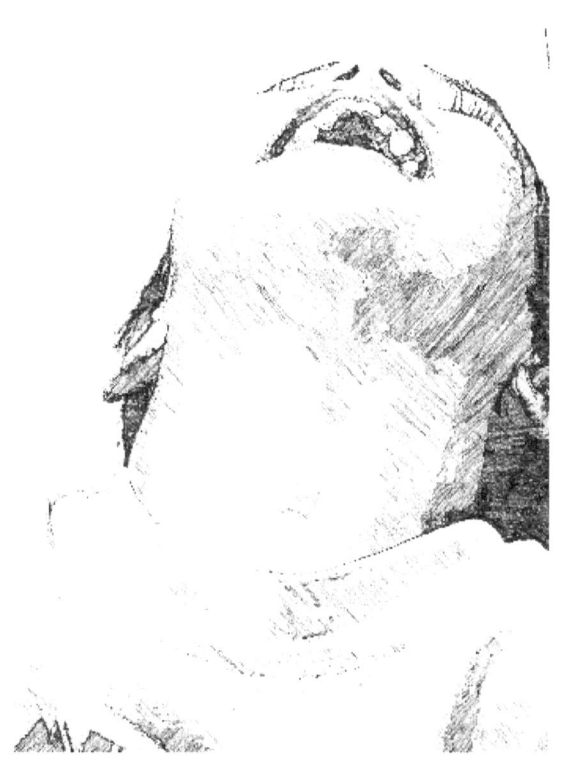

After the parade was over, Kyle grabbed his skateboard and they rode to the beach. Kyle loved going to the beach. He showed her how he boogie boards, while she laid out enjoying the sea breeze on the sand.

After the beach, Kyle took Rosie for a bike ride. They went all over the neighborhood and back. She even met a couple of his buddies from school along the way. She was the happiest spider around.

Kyle also took Rosie fishing at the lake by his house. She's never done so many things before in one day. Kyle taught her how to fish and Rosie caught the biggest fish Kyle had ever seen. They both were so excited.

Since it was getting late in the day, Kyle took Rosie back to her web that was up in the tree and before Rosie climbed down from Kyle's arm, she gently kissed Kyle on the cheek. Kyle replied before going home; "You made me feel a lot better. I had so much fun with you today". Rosie replied back; "I had the best time of my life with you".

"Rosie"? Kyle asked. "Yes"? Rosie answered. Kyle said smiling; "You're a great friend. I will see you tomorrow". Then Kyle gave her a small kiss and rode home.

Rosie sat on the branch of the tree and sweetly smiled watching her new friend Kyle ride off as a tear ran down her face as she finally felt content.

She was truly the happiest spider in town.
And she really did live happily ever after.

The End